CROWDFUNDING

Published in the United States of America by Cherry Lake Publishing
Ann Arbor, Michigan
www.cherrylakepublishing.com

Content Adviser: Marcus Collins, MBA, Chief Consumer Connections Officer, Marketing Professor
Reading Adviser: Marla Conn MS, Ed., Literacy specialist, Read-Ability, Inc.

Photo Credits: © Photoraidz/Shutterstock.com, Cover, 1; © Billion Photos/Shutterstock.com, Cover, 1; © Oleg Golovnev/
Shutterstock.com, 5; © DFP Photographic/Shutterstock.com, 6; © Robert Kneschke/Shutterstock.com, 8; © Imfoto/
Shutterstock.com, 11; © Dragon Images/Shutterstock.com, 13; © Tatiana Chekryzhova/Shutterstock.com, 14;
© Dusan Petkovic/Shutterstock.com, 17; © mark reinstein/Shutterstock.com, 18; © Mike_shots/Shutterstock.com, 20;
© wavebreakmedia/Shutterstock.com, 23; © Sergey Novikov/Shutterstock.com, 24; © Featureflash Photo Agency/
Shutterstock.com, 26; © YAKOBCHUK VIACHESLAV/Shutterstock.com, 28

Library of Congress Cataloging-in-Publication Data

Names: Orr, Tamra, author.
Title: Crowdfunding / Tamra B. Orr.
Description: [Ann Arbor, MI] : Cherry Lake Publishing, [2019] | Series: Global citizens : social media | Audience: Grade 4 to 6. |
    Includes bibliographical references and index.
Identifiers: LCCN 2018035592 | ISBN 9781534143104 (hardcover) | ISBN 9781534139664 (pbk.) | ISBN 9781534140868 (pdf) |
    ISBN 9781534142060 (hosted ebook)
Subjects: LCSH: Electronic fund raising. | Crowd funding.
Classification: LCC HG177 .O77 2019 | DDC 658.15/224—dc23
LC record available at https://lccn.loc.gov/2018035592

Cherry Lake Publishing would like to acknowledge the work of the Partnership for 21st Century Learning.
Please visit www.p21.org for more information.

Printed in the United States of America
Corporate Graphics

ABOUT THE AUTHOR

Tamra Orr is the author of more than 500 nonfiction books for readers of all ages. A graduate of Ball State University, she now lives in the Pacific Northwest with her family. When she isn't writing books, she is either camping, reading, or on the computer researching the latest topic.

TABLE OF CONTENTS

CHAPTER 1

History: Global Fund-raising

Think about something you really want that you don't have the money for. It happens to everyone. That something might be a new bike or a new guitar. It might be tickets to a concert or to Comic-Con. It might even be something that someone you care about needs, such as a better wheelchair for a family member or help with medical costs for a friend. Your allowance helps. That babysitting or lawn-care money you earned helps, too, but it might not be enough. What do you do? You could ask your family and friends if they would be willing to donate a few dollars to your cause. Or, thanks to **crowdfunding** and social media, you could ask the whole world.

Alexander Pope gave a shout-out in his book to the 750 people
who helped fund his project in 1713.

Back in Time

In the late 1990s and early 2000s during the rise of the internet,
crowdfunding became the quickest way to raise money. But that's
not when it got its start. Crowdfunding has been around since
at least the 18th century—well before the internet. (The term
crowdfunding, however, wasn't coined until 2006 by Michael Sullivan.)
Alexander Pope, a famous poet during the time, asked people to

Marillion's 12th studio album is said to have been the first modern-day crowdfunded project.

help fund his project of translating German poetry to English. In return, Pope promised to include their names in his work. Wolfgang Amadeus Mozart also used crowdfunding strategies to pay for his concerts. Back then, it was a slow process. It often took years to raise the necessary funds.

Crowdfunding and the Internet

In 1997, Marillion, a British rock band, successfully raised money from people all over the world in order to fund its tour. The band used the internet, only 6 years old at the time, to raise $60,000—

making Marillion the pioneers of modern crowdfunding. Three years later, the first crowdfunding site, ArtistShare, launched. ArtistShare was the first website dedicated to raising money for musicians looking for ways to fund their next project. The novel idea of using the internet to raise money from fans and interested parties quickly spread. Soon more websites like ArtistShare started popping up. From big music stars and franchises to **entrepreneurs**, people of all backgrounds use crowdfunding platforms to market their ideas and inventions to the entire world.

Timeline of Crowdfunding Sites

Company	Launch Year
ArtistShare	2000
Kiva	2005
Mightycause (formerly Razoo)	2006
Indiegogo; peerbackers	2008
Kickstarter; Optimize Capital Markets (Canada)	2009
GoFundMe; RocketHub	2010
Fundable	2012

Many successful start-ups got their start on Kickstarter or other similar crowdfunding platforms.

Welcome to the 21st Century

In 2008, Indiegogo launched. This website focused on a reward-based structure in order to **incentivize** people to donate and to donate more. Reward-based crowdfunding involves people contributing money to a fund in return for some kind of reward. The more money people give, the bigger the reward. Since then, crowdfunding has done nothing but grow. In 2015, the crowdfunding industry raised $34 billion worldwide. Experts predict that by 2025, that number will be closer to $300 billion!

Developing Questions

Before modern-day crowdfunding, start-up businesses and entrepreneurs raised money one of three ways. They would request a loan from a bank, try to network with the right people, or hope a **venture capitalist** *or* **angel investor** *would give them money. This process was hit-or-miss. Banks don't always give out loans, and when they do, sometimes the amount isn't enough. And meeting someone with enough money to help fund an expensive project doesn't happen every day! That's why crowdfunding fills a need. One way to launch a successful crowdfunding campaign is to use social media. Social media platforms, like Instagram, Facebook, and Twitter, can help promote your campaign. What other ways can you successfully run a crowdfunding campaign?*

Geography: Donations Near and Far

People all over the world have dreams, hopes, and needs. Many of them have participated in or have started a crowdfunding campaign. Crowdfunding connects people from all across the world. The majority of the money donated to these campaigns comes from North America ($17.2 billion), closely followed by Asia ($10.5 billion) and Europe ($6.48 billion). Many countries even have their own crowdfunding sites, such as Canada's Optimize Capital Markets, the Netherland's Geldvoorelkaar, and Kenya's Babandu. Let's take a closer look at a few of these areas.

Sweden-based Tessin is a crowdfunding platform that serves the real estate industry.

Malaysia

Crowdfunding in Asia has grown rapidly. In 2015, it grew twice as much as in Africa, Europe, or North America. Malaysia, specifically, is taking advantage of this growth. As of May 2018, the Malaysian federal debt had reached about $337 billion! Worried about her country, 27-year-old Nik Shazarina Bakti set up a crowdfunding campaign on GoGetFunding to help reduce the debt.

Kenya

Crowdfunding is not a foreign concept in Kenya. In fact, the people there have a word for it: *harambee*, which means "pulling and working together" in Swahili. Harambee is a guiding principle in the Kenyan culture. So it's no wonder that there are several successful Kenya-based crowdfunding platforms, including M-Changa and the Kenya Climate Innovation Center.

Most Popular Platforms

Crowdfunding sites tend to come and go like any other website. But others have stuck around, and as of early 2018, these are the ones used most often for crowdfunding:

1. *Kickstarter*
2. *Indiegogo*
3. *GoFundMe*
4. *Mightycause*
5. *RocketHub*

KissKissBankBank, a France-based crowdfunding platform for creative projects, launched in 2009. In 2017, campaigns on the platform had a 70 percent success rate!

Women-led campaigns in the Middle East have about a 29 percent higher average promised amount compared to men-led campaigns in the same region.

Women in the Middle East

Across the world, women are generally more likely to reach their funding goal than men. In fact, women are 32 percent more successful than men in reaching their goal. This is true for women in the Middle East as well. According to reports, women there were 4 percent more successful than men in reaching their crowdfunding goal.

Gathering and Evaluating Sources

One of the best ways to learn how to do something well is to research people who have succeeded at the same goal. Spend some time online looking at the most successful crowdfunding campaigns. Analyze what these campaigns did, what they have in common, and what made them unique from the others. Evaluate whether these elements could be applied to a crowdfunding idea you might have.

CHAPTER 3

Civics:
The Legal Issue

Crowdfunding is a new form of earning money for anything from plane tickets to lifesaving surgery to everything in between. It gives people the chance to plead their cause, their need, their product, or their services—and see if the public responds. It gives a voice to people who might typically be overlooked and unheard, and a chance for them to achieve a dream, whatever it may be. Crowdfunding has gotten so popular that laws have been passed to further help entrepreneurs and businesses succeed, but also to protect individuals with big hearts from getting scammed.

Small businesses should be aware that unless they file a patent or copyright, their campaign to launch a creative idea could potentially be copied by others.

President Obama said that the JOBS Act "is a potential game changer." According to the act, entrepreneurs are now able to raise up to $1 million!

Thanks, President Obama

In April 2012, President Barack Obama made many small business owners very happy when he signed the Jumpstart Our Business Startups Act, or JOBS Act. This bill was designed to help small business owners and entrepreneurs raise more funds through processes like crowdfunding. Thanks to this bill, any investor can give a business money in return for **equity** in that business. Ever since 1933, only very wealthy investors were allowed to invest in new small businesses. Now anyone, regardless of their income or **net worth**, is allowed to contribute money. The first part of the act went into effect in 2013 and the second part in 2016. At the signing ceremony, Obama stated, "One of the great things about America is that we're a nation of doers. We think big, take risks, and believe that anyone with a solid plan and a willingness to work hard can take even the most improbable idea and turn it into a solid business."

Developing Claims and Using Evidence

Deciding which side of an argument you fall on can be difficult. Consider this argument: Should there be any rules about who can use crowdfunding? Go online and research people's thoughts on this. For example, should wealthy people be allowed to launch campaigns even if they already have the financial means to achieve their goals? Why or why not? If an income limit is to be established for those who launch crowdfunding campaigns, what should the limit be and who should determine it? Research this topic further using your local library and the internet. Gather the information you find to support your answers.

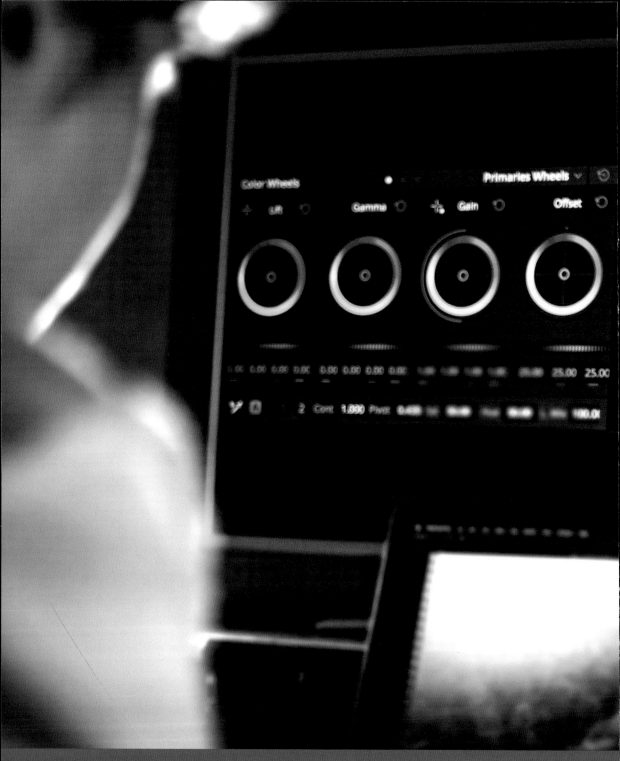

If you're creating a promotional video for your crowdfunding campaign, make sure the music is free to use for commercial purposes!

Protecting Your Savings

Now everyday people, and not just the wealthy, can reap the potential rewards if a company or start-up does well. But the U.S. Securities and Exchange Commission (SEC) and the Financial Industry Regulatory Authority (FINRA) have put rules in place to protect investors. According to the SEC and FINRA, if a crowdfund investor has less than $100,000 in a bank account, that person can only invest up to 5 percent of their money or $2,000, whichever is greater. If a crowdfund investor has $100,000 or more in the bank, that person can only contribute up to 10 percent of their **income**. These rules are in place to protect everyday people from investing all their life savings and potentially losing it all!

CHAPTER 4

Economics: New Jobs and Companies

Fans of the *Veronica Mars* television series . . .

A young man in Tanzania who loves outer space . . .

A man who walks 21 miles a day to work and then back again . . .

A young girl whose grandfather has Parkinson's disease . . .

A teenager who struggles with mental illness . . .

What do all of these people have in common? All of them launched crowdfunding campaigns to achieve their goals. Some wanted to make a movie and some wanted an education. Some sought investors and some wanted a car. And some just wanted a chance. Each one reached out to the online community and hoped that strangers around the globe would reach back and lend a helping hand.

Experts believe that by 2025, the crowdfunding industry
could potentially grow to $93 billion!

Choices, Choices

Crowdfunding is a potential way for a person to get money,
but it is not necessarily easy. It takes time and effort. Typically,
the more attention the site is given, the higher the likelihood
of success.

First, people need to choose which funding site to use. There are
several factors to keep in mind when making this choice. For example,
Kickstarter is the most popular site, with more than $1.4 billion

Crowdfunding campaigns not only could help fund a young person's tuition for summer camp, but also improve the camp itself!

in **pledges** and 7.5 million backers since it began in 2009. Kickstarter is considered the best choice for artists, dancers, designers, filmmakers, chefs, musicians, photographers, and actors. The platform focuses on art-oriented campaigns. Before a campaign is accepted on Kickstarter, a committee reads over the proposal to make sure it is a good fit.

Nonprofit campaigns are not found on Kickstarter. Instead, they tend to be listed on Indiegogo, the second most popular crowdfunding site. Indiegogo does not filter its projects. There is no committee to get past. GoFundMe specializes in emergency-based campaigns ("Please help us get the money to build a wheelchair ramp at our house") and short-term personal projects ("Help me go to Africa to represent my high school at a climate change conference"). In 2016, this site raised more than $5 million for victims in the Pulse night club shooting in Orlando, Florida. Mightycause also focuses on nonprofits and specific causes, while RocketHub is used more by investors rather than random donors.

Time for Camp!

Since GoFundMe started in 2010, it reports it has helped young people raise more than $4.3 million to go to summer camp. Between 2013 and 2014, that number tripled and continues to grow.

In mid-2018, Kylie Jenner fans created a GoFundMe to help Jenner with the last $100 million she needed to become the world's youngest self-made billionaire.

The Best of the Best

What crowdfunding campaigns have earned the most money? In early 2018, that record was held by Pebble Time, a smartwatch designed to keep track of a person's life longer and better than its competitor, Apple. During its campaign, more than 78,000 people donated, for a total of $20.3 million! (The company's goal was only $500,000.) Pledges of $159 or more resulted in a reward of a watch. Pebble Time followed its first campaign with a second one for a heart rate enabled watch with a built-in GPS and music. More than 66,000 backers contributed $12.8 million.

Communicating Conclusions

Before you read this book, had you ever started an online fundraiser or contributed to one? Has what you have learned changed how you see crowdfunding? Share what you have learned with others. Go online and explore various online campaigns, from nonprofits to businesses to personal needs. Take time to analyze what makes each campaign more or less appealing or persuasive. Which ones do you respond to the most and why?

As of May 2018, there have been $3.6 billion pledged to various projects on Kickstarter—including many popular video games!

Another huge success was the Coolest Cooler. It not only kept food cold, but also featured a blender, waterproof Bluetooth speaker, and USB charger. During its campaign, over 62,000 people donated $12.3 million. Prizes ranged from a reusable plastic party cup with the company's logo ($25) to a promise from the inventor to come to your next event and serve your guests from the cooler ($2,000 and up).

Jobs

The impact of crowdfunding reaches far beyond the people campaigning and donating. According to a report, Kickstarter alone has created more than 300,000 part-time and full-time jobs, as well as 8,800 new companies and nonprofits. All of these new businesses and jobs have resulted in an estimated $5.3 billion in additional economic activity.

Taking Informed Action

Spend time reading different people's campaigns. Find one that you think is a really worthy cause. While it is not necessary to donate to it, why not spread the word about it? More than half of the campaigns that are emailed to other people result in donations. Twelve percent of Facebook shares and 3 percent of Twitter shares turn into someone donating. Reach out and help any way you can.

Think About It

A study done on the success of various crowdfunding campaigns revealed that just about half of them succeed in hitting their financial goals. Of those that do, an amazing 78 percent go on to exceed those goals. The average campaign gets $7,000 in a 9-week period. Most successful campaigns have descriptions that fall between 300 and 500 words, frequently update their supporters with news, and have a marketing plan. Those with videos raise 105 percent more than those that do not. What do these facts tell you about crowdfunding?

For More Information

FURTHER READING

Lebrun, Jean-Luc. *The Grant Writing and Crowdfunding Guide for Young Investigators in Science.* Hackensack, NJ: World Scientific, 2017.

Mapua, Jeff. *Making the Most of Crowdfunding.* New York: Rosen Central, 2015.

Paisley, Erinne. *Can Your Smartphone Change the World?* Custer, WA: Orca Book Publishers, 2017.

WEBSITES

National Theatre for Student Artists—How to Crowdfund for Summer Camp
www.nationalstudenttheatre.org/news/2018/how-to-crowdfund-for-summer-camp
Want to go to summer camp but don't have enough money? Forget the bake sale! Learn how to fund your way to camp with this easy how-to post!

TeenBusiness—Teen Crowdfunding Campaigns from Top Crowdfunding Sources
www.teenbusiness.com/crowd-funding-campaigns
Read about the many young entrepreneurs who are using crowdfunding platforms to fund their projects!

GLOSSARY

angel investor (AYN-juhl in-VES-tur) wealthy person who invests a large amount of money in a new business or start-up

crowdfunding (KROUD-fuhnd-ing) the practice of getting funding by asking for money from a large number of people, especially from the online community

entrepreneurs (ahn-truh-pruh-NURZ) people who organize, manage, and assume the risks of a business

equity (EK-wih-tee) ownership right in a business

incentivize (in-SEN-tih-vize) to provide something that makes a person do something, like donate more money to a crowdfunding campaign

income (IN-kuhm) the money that a person earns or receives, usually from working

net worth (NET WURTH) how much a person owns (assets) minus what the person owes to others (liabilities or debt)

nonprofit (nahn-PRAH-fit) an organization that does business without the purpose of making a profit

pledges (PLEJ-iz) money given as a promise

venture capitalist (VEN-chur KAP-ih-tuh-list) a person or business that invests in a start-up or new business

INDEX

[21ST CENTURY SKILLS LIBRARY]